Anonymous

**Genealogy of Judge John Taylor and his descendants**

Anonymous

**Genealogy of Judge John Taylor and his descendants**

ISBN/EAN: 9783337735692

Printed in Europe, USA, Canada, Australia, Japan

Cover: Foto ©ninafisch / pixelio.de

More available books at **www.hansebooks.com**

# Genealogy

OF

# JUDGE JOHN TAYLOR

## AND HIS DESCENDANTS.

DETROIT, MICH.:

THE RICHMOND & BACKUS CO., STATIONERS AND PRINTERS,

1886.

"Remember the days of old, consider the years of many generations : Ask thy father and he will shew thee ; thy elders and they will tell thee."—DEUT. 32, 7.

_____

"It is an honorable instinct that prompts men to perpetuate the memory of their forefathers : and to preserve from the decay which overtakes all physical nature, those acts and characteristics which spring from the soul and like it are capable of immortality,"

_____

# THE GENEALOGY

## OF

# JUDGE JOHN TAYLOR,

### OF SARATOGA CO., NEW YORK,

BORN AUGUST 25, 1749, DIED APRIL 26, 1829,

### AND HIS DESCENDANTS.

_____

THE name of the family of Taylor, which settled in Middletown, New Jersey, in the latter part of seventeenth century—1692—had been subject to the mutations and corruptions so often met with in ancient families. The ancestor (according to Burke) was the Norman Baron Taillefer, who accompanied William the Conqueror, and had a position near his person in his invasion of England, and fell in his presence in the van of his army at the battle of Hastings, on Saturday, October 14, 1066.

Bulwer, in "The Last of the Saxon Kings," thus describes his death : In the midst of the Duke William's cohort was the sacred gonfanon (standard), and in front of it, and of the whole line, rode a bold warrior of gigantic height, and as he rode

> Chanting aloud the lusty strain
> Of Rolland and of Charlemagne,
> And the dead who deathless are
> Who fell at famous Roncesvalles.

He seemed beside himself with the joy of battle. As he rode, and as he chanted, he threw up his sword in the air like a glee-man, catching it nimbly as it fell, and flourishing it wildly, till, as if unable to restrain his fierce exhilaration, he put spurs to his horse and dashing forward to the front of the detachment of Saxon riders, he shouted,

" A Taillefer ! A Taillefer !!" and by voice
and gesture challenged forth some one to
single combat. A fiery young thegn (soldier) started forth and crossing swords with
him, Taillefer, again throwing up and catching his sword with incredible rapidity, shore
the unhappy Saxon from the helm to the
chine, and riding over his corpse, shouting
and laughing, he again renewed his chal-
lenge. A second rode forward and shared
the same fate. The rest of the English
horsemen stared at each other aghast. Leo-
fivine, the Saxon King's brother, came in
front of the detachment, and not drawing
his sword, but with his spear raised over his
head, and his body covered by his shield.
Taillefer rushed forward, his sword shivered
on the Saxon shield, and in the same mo-
ment he fell a corpse under the hoofs of his
steed, transfixed by the Saxon's spear. A
cry of woe, in which even William joined
his deep voice, wailed through the Norman
ranks.

Taillefer's family received from the Conqueror large landed estates in the county of Kent, England, as his portion of the spoils. Hanger Taylefer, his descendant, held lands in the tenure of Ospringe, county of Kent, A. D. 1256, and from him about one hundred years later, we have John Taylor in the homestall in Schodoschurst, county of Kent, and from him the possession is perfectly traced through William, John, William, John, John, John, Mathew to Edward the Emigrant. William Taylor, son of John of the homestall (homestead) in Schodoschurst, was living in the time of King Richard II., Henry IV., and Henry V. (1377 to 1422), and was succeeded by his son John Taylor of Schodoschurst, who died about the fifth year of Edward IV., and was succeeded by his son William of Schodoschurst, who married Joane, daughter of Henry Gibban, and died 1493. He was succeeded by his son John Taylor, in the time of Richard III. and Henry VII. (1483 to 1508), who married Margaret, daughter and sole heir of Humphrey de Fairsted, and acquired the estates and arms of De Fairsted. His son John married Thomasine, daughter of John Isaac of Levington, Sussex county. He died 1560, leaving daughter Alice and a son, John Taylor, who was Lord of the Manor of Schodoschurst, three of whose descendants became barons. Thomas created a baron January 16, 1665 ; his son Sir Thomas, born August 10, 1657, died 1696, left an only child, Sir Thomas, born 1693, died 1720, unmarried, and the barony became extinct. John Taylor, Lord of the Manor of Schodoschurst, married Elizabeth Chute, daughter of Philip of Bethersden, county of Kent, and had a son, Mathew Taylor, who settled in Sussex county. By his first marriage he had son Mathew, born A. D. 1591, who had a daughter, Margaret, born 1634, and married Thomas White, in 1656. They left a son, John White. For his second wife Mathew

Taylor married Margaret, only daughter and heiress of Richard Freeland, Esq., and acquired the Freeland Estate and Arms. He was succeeded by his son, John Taylor, born in 1611, died in 1683. He left two sons, Mathew and Edward Taylor, (of both hereafter.)

John Stringer of Old Romney, married Alice, daughter of John Taylor, Lord of the Manor of Schodoschurst, Their daughter, Susan, married Sir Thomas Scott of Scott's Hall. Their son, Edward Scott, married Lady Catherine, daughter of George, Earl of Norwich, and left a son, Sir Thomas Scott, who married Catherine, daughter of Sir George Carteret, proprietor of East New Jersey, under whose influence the Taylor family acquired large landed estates in Monmouth county, in that colony.

Charles II. of England, in 1664, gave to his brother James, the Duke of York, all the territory where the Dutch and Swedes had settled, a part of which was New Jersey

—then called New Albion by the English. James sold his right to New Albion to Sir George Carteret, a noble cavalier, who had fought for the crown, and it was then named New Jersey in honor of a gallant defense of the Isle of Jersey, in the English Channel, where Carteret had commanded.

Mathew Taylor, born 1655, the son of John Taylor, born 1611, was engaged with his cousin, John White, at New York, in purchasing lands, in New Jersey, from the Indians, through the influence of his connection with Sir George Carteret. A deed, dated November 19, 1681, conveys from Powark, Cowalamuck, and other Indians, to the Lady Carteret, in trust for Mathew Taylor of New York, and others, a large tract of land in Somerset county, being in depth four miles on both sides of the north branch of the Raritan river, at its junction with the south branch. Mathew Taylor died in 1688, and by his last will, made in 1687, bequeathed his property to his brother

Edward, then residing in London. He bequeathed ten guineas to his friend J. Manning, to buy a mourning ring.

Middletown township, Monmouth county, New Jersey, lies along the southern shore of Raritan bay, and originally extended from and including Sandy Hook to near the mouth of Raritan river, and extending eight or ten miles back southerly from the shore. It was in the roadstead within Sandy Hook that Hendrick Hudson, in the Dutch yacht "Half Moon," came to anchor on the third day of September, 1609. The verdant shore and the picturesque and richly crested hills of Middletown first attracted his attention on entering the ·bay of Raritan, and it was on the shore of Middletown that he first landed. Jouet, his mate, in his published journal, pronounced it "very good land to fall in with, and very pleasant land to see," and therein Jouet showed his good judgment and taste, for it is, indeed, "the land of every land the pride." The famous " Concessions " of the lords proprietors of East New Jersey, in favor of "all and every of the adventurers, and all such as shall settle and plant there," directed the attention of many intelligent settlers in adjacent parts to that region, and a number of reputable families becoming acquainted with the fertility of the soil and salubrity of the climate, moved there in 1664–5–6, and made settlements in Middletown. Their descendants still form a considerable portion of the population of that region. The celebrated "Stout tradition" gives six white families as settled on the site of the present village of Middletown in 1648.

[1]EDWARD TAYLOR came over from London in 1692 and settled at Garrets' Hill, where his descendants, in 1880, still occupied a portion of the land he then acquired. Garrets' Hill, so designated from the first

---

NOTE.—Nos. 1 to 9 shows the generation of that person.

settlement of the country, but in later years called by the pilots "Pigeon Hill," is a prominent landmark seen from all parts of the lower harbor of New York. It is a round top regular knoll, rising high above the adjacent land, and for many years beyond the memory of the present generation had a single scraggy cedar tree on its crown, being otherwise entirely bare. It is situated about two miles easterly from the village of Middletown. The old Taylor homestead mansion, built in 1729 by George, son of the Emigrant, stands close under the hill on the easterly side, and in 1876 was occupied by a lineal descendant of "the first man." It was then in good condition, still exhibiting the old pictured Dutch tiles in the fireplace and other characteristics of the early day in which it was erected, and interesting too, as a memorial of the hardy race it has sheltered for over a century and a-half.

[1]EDWARD TAYLOR, the Emigrant son of John and Mary, born about 1650, married

Catherine —. He was called "of Briggs House, York county, England, residing in London." Having succeeded to the property of his brother Mathew, in New Jersey, who died 1688, and having himself made purchases of land in the vicinity of Garrets' Hill, he came over with his family and settled there in 1692. He appears from the records to have made additional purchases of land in that vicinity, and became a large land holder. There he died. Scraps of manuscript, apparently in his handwriting, give the date of birth of his children thus : [2]Edward, August 8, 1678 ; Hannah, January 16, 1680 ; George, December 16, 1684 ; [2]William, October 25, 1688 ; John, June 19, 16— (manuscript imperfect) ; [2]Joseph, probably born in New Jersey.

GEORGE succeeded to his father's estate at Garrets' Hill and, in 1729, erected the old homestead now there. John and Joseph appear to have remained at Middletown. [2]Edward and [2]William settled in the upper part of Monmouth county, at Colts Neck, in town of Freehold. Many of the descendants went to the " new country " in the State of New York and in the State of Ohio, and thence have removed to western and southern cities and States, and most of them have become useful, prosperous citizens of good character—some of them filling places of distinction. None of them, so far as we can learn, have ever been convicted of a crime under the laws of their country. [2]William married Hannah Grover, settled in Freehold, had ten children : [3]Edward, Safety, William, Deborah, Hannah, Catherine and Martha (twins), Rebecca, [3]Mercy (our maternal ancestor), and Esther.

[3]MERCY, born December, 1728, married Col. Richard Cox, born March, 1727, who was afterward an honored officer in the Revolutionary War. They had nine children : Richard, William, Thomas, Joshua, John, James, [4]Chloe, born May, 1752 (our ancestor, wife of Judge John Taylor of

Saratoga county, New York), Rebecca, and Polly. Six of them married and had children. [3]Mercy Cox lived a widow with her children twenty-two years; was remarkable for strong, tenacious memory. Her last years were spent with her daughter [4]Chloe, at the home of Judge John Taylor, in Charlton, Saratoga county, New York, and she died there in February, 1827, aged ninety-nine years. Their son, [4]Richard Cox, was a major in the Jersey Line in the Revolutionary War, for which service he received a grant of land in the State of Ohio, upon which he settled and reared a family. [4]Thomas Cox went to Kentucky. His children, Thomas, Charles, Harriet, and Betsey, were kind, generous, hospitable Kentuckians. [4]James Cox settled in Kentucky, on a plantation near Versailles, and died there at the age of 93. Hon. S. S. Cox, for many years member of Congress from the city of New York, and more recently minister of United States to Turkey, is said to be a descendant of the father of Col. Richard Cox, above named.

²Edward Taylor, our paternal ancestor, eldest son of the Emigrant, who settled at Colt's Neck, in Freehold, married Catherine Morford. They had eleven children: Edward, ³Joseph, our paternal ancestor, George, John, Thomas, James, Hannah, Susan, Esther, Catharine, and Rebecca. ²Edward, by his will, gave to his eldest son a silver mug brought by his father from England, which was said to have been a complimentary award for some special service. It was reported that the mug had been melted down and a modern cup made of it, but we have been informed that the mug is safe in the possession of ⁶Edward Taylor of Upper Freehold, the sixth Edward from and including the Emigrant. His father, Doctor E. Taylor, was an eminent quaker of Upper Freehold, and superintended the Friends Asylum, near Frankford, Pa., from 1823 to 1832, when his wife died,

and he returned to his farm in Freehold,
where he died. He was converted to that
religion by his wife, who was a noted
preacher. He has numerous descendants.
One [6]son removed to Memphis, Tennessee,
and [6]James to Cincinnati, Ohio.

[3]JOSEPH TAYLOR, our paternal ancestor,
born March, 1720, died 1766, lived at Upper
Freehold, N. J., married Elizabeth Ashton,
and had eight children : Joseph, [4]William,
[4]John (our ancestor, born August, 1749, and
died April, 1829), Elisha, Sally, Elizabeth,
[4]Catherine, and [4]Lydia, who married Major
John Porter of the army.

[4]JOSEPH moved to Ohio, and raised a large
family. [4]William, born about 1747, removed
to Bainbridge, Ross county, Ohio, married
Lucy Embry, and had fourteen children :
Joseph, William, Edward, David, John,
George, Elisha, Isaac, Jonathan, Mary,
Sarah, Eleanor, Lucy, Elizabeth.

[4]JOHN TAYLOR (whose genealogy we
record), born at Upper Freehold, N. J.,

1749, married Chloe Cox, born May, 1752, an earnest Christian, noted for her cheerfulness and industry. They moved to the "new country," in the State of New York, and settled in Charlton, Saratoga county, in 1774. He and Judge Childs were the Judges of the County Court from 1809 to 1818, inclusive, He was a member of the legislature of the State of New York, a Presbyterian, and a prominent and useful citizen, and died at the age of eighty years, at Ballston Spa, at the home of his son, Hon. John W. Taylor, his mental faculties and physical powers but little impaired. He had nine children: [5]Joseph, born 1775, died 1829; [5]Richard, born 1777, died 1847; [5]William, born 1779, died 1836; [5]Edward, born 1781, died 1866; [5]John W., born 1784, died 1854; [5]Elisha, born 1786, died 1861; [5]Elizabeth or Betsey, born 1788, and still living, in 1886, with her son, a Baptist clergyman, Rev. John T. Seeley, D.D,, near Rochester, N. Y. ; [5]Sally, born 1792, and still living, in 1886, with her daughter, at Wilson, N. Y. ; and ⁵Anna, born 1794, died 1840.

⁴CATHERINE married Joseph Braiden, and two of their grand-daughters, ⁶Ann Lyons and ⁶Emma Lyons married W. S. Derrick and A. H. Derrick, of the State Department, Washington, who performed important service relative to the Ashburton Treaty. Their posterity are in the Southern States.

⁴LYDIA, who married Major John Porter of the army, was left a widow and died in 1825. Her last years were spent with her nephew, ⁵William Taylor, born 1779, at his home in Charlton, Saratoga county, N. Y., and she bequeathed the last eight hundred dollars of her property to her said nephew, for the collegiate education of his son, ⁶Elisha, born May 14, 1817.

ELIZABETH ASHTON, the widow of ³Joseph Taylor, and mother of Judge ⁴John Taylor, refused many offers of second marriage, also invitations from her sons to live with them in Ohio and in New York. She said, "Let me live on the land endeared to me by my husband's home, die his widow, and lie by his side in my grave.' Devoting herself to the care of her children, to hospitality and to charity, she lived for fifty years on her dower estate, a graceful, pious, venerated and beloved matron. Only five of her children lived to have issue, but her posterity in 1875 numbered over 500 souls, and none born with any deformity, destitute of common sense, or convicted of any offense against the laws of the land.

### CHILDREN AND GRAND-CHILDREN OF JUDGE 4JOHN TAYLOR.

5JOSEPH TAYLOR, born 1775, died 1829, married Mary Henry, had two children, 6Mary Jane and 6John Cox. He was a merchant, and finally he was appointed to a confidential position in the United States

Post Office Department, at Washington,
D. C., and continued there during the
remainder of his life, and died and was
buried at Hagerstown, New Jersey. His
daughter, Mary Jane, never married. She
was an intelligent, successful teacher. She
was appointed to a position in Post Office
Department, and died at Washington, D. C.,
in 1872, leaving about six thousand dollars
by will to her friends.

[6]John Cox Taylor, son of [5]Joseph, born
1815, died 1836, was a capable, scholarly
young man. He graduated at Union College, Schenectady, N. Y., at the age of
seventeen years, read law in Washington,
went to Huntsville, Alabama, was admitted
to the bar before he was twenty-one years
of age, but was accidentally drowned in
attempting to ford Cotoco Creek on horseback. He was greatly beloved by his friends
and was a very popular, promising young
man. On his table, after his death, was
found the following impromptu lines:

When the song and the dance are smiling around,
And the heart heaves no sigh,
Talk not to me then of life's narrow bound—
Let me not die!

When the thunder is booming along the storm cloud,
And the lightning is high,
Unfold not for me the burial shroud—
Let me not die!

When the sun shines bright upon the glad earth,
And the merry birds fly;
When the heart gushes forth in its joy and its mirth—
Let me not die!

But when sunset and stillness are breathing around,
O'er earth and o'er sky,
Then! Oh, then, let my death knell sound—
Then let me die!

At the twilight time bright spirits have power,
And fair angels are nigh:
Soul, take thy flight in that hallowed hour—
Then let me die!


[5]RICHARD TAYLOR, farmer, born April,
1777, died August, 1847, married Miss —
Hawley, of Charlton, Saratoga county.
One son survived, [6]Anson Hawley Taylor.

His second wife, Mrs. Holmes, a widow,
had one child, [6]Obadiah, died in youth. His
third wife, Sophia Wright, had two children :
[6]John Wright Taylor, and [6]Chloe Sophia
Taylor. His fourth wife was Mrs. Phoebe
Clark, a widow. They had children :
[6]Elisha E. Leech Taylor and [6]James Monroe
Taylor. The former became a prominent
Baptist clergyman, and the latter a large
manufacturer in the cities of Brooklyn and
New York of the various products from
potash. [5]Richard Taylor, writing to his
cousin, [5]James Cox of Versailles, Ky., in
1799, says that fifteen feet of snow had
fallen that winter in Charlton, Saratoga
county, N. Y. That at one storm it fell
three feet deep without drifting. Also he
records that in August, 1816, a very remarkable hail storm occurred, and the next day
the hail stones could be shoveled up in
wagon loads.

[5]WILLIAM TAYLOR, born 1779, died 1836,
was a farmer, justice of the peace, super-

visor of the town of Charlton, and an elder in the Presbyterian Church. He married Lucy Harger. They had thirteen children : [6]James Edwin, born September, 1807 ; [6]William Lorenzo, November, 1808 ; [6]Eber Leander, June, 1810 ; [6]Ann Elizabeth, February, 1812 ; [6]Sarah Sophia, February, 1814 ; [6]John, July, 1815 ; [6]Elisha, May, 1817 ; [6]Samuel, 1819 ; [6]David, 1821 ; [6]Richard, 1823 ; [6]Josiah, 1825 ; Lydia Lucy Jane, May, 1827 ; [6]Joseph Elliott, June, 1829. [5]William resided in Charlton all his life. He visited the State of Michigan, in 1836, and purchased a large farm and other lands, intending to remove to that State. On his return home he died suddenly of apoplexy, in September, 1836, leaving his widow and ten children surviving.

[5]EDWARD TAYLOR, farmer, born February, 1781, died December, 1866, married Eunice Curtis. Their children were [6]John Orville, born 1808 ; [6]Ann Maria, 1810 ; [6]Luzern Curtis, 1812 ; [6]Phebe Eliza, 1814 ; [6]Elisha

Cox, 1816; [6]William Andrew, 1818; [6]Jane Caroline, 1821; [6]Eunice Clara, 1825; [6]Sarah Elizabeth, 1827; [6]Susan Patience, 1830. [5]Edward Taylor resided in Charlton most of his life. He was an officer in the army during the war of 1812. He was fond of good horses, and raised fine stock. He died at Gloverville, N. Y.

[5]JOHN W. TAYLOR, born March 26, 1784, and died 1854, graduated from Union College, Schenectady, N. Y., 1803, as valadictorian of his class, organized Ballston Centre Academy that year, attorney-at-law 1807; married Jane Hodge of Albany, N. Y., 1806 (a beautiful woman, attractive, courageous, practical, efficient, with great delicacy and tact. She died 1838); justice of the peace in 1808, and State commissioner of loans at Ballston Spa, Saratoga county, N. Y.; member of the legislature of New York, 1811–12—vigorous supporter of the War of 1812 with Great Britain. He was member of Congress uninterruptedly twenty

years, from 1813 to 1833, both inclusive, was speaker of the House of Representatives in the sixteenth and again in the nineteenth Congress. On the admission of Missouri he delivered the first speech ever made in Congress squarely opposing the extension of slavery. He was a practical man of good judgment, experience, observation and decision, and was often consulted in national affairs by Presidents Madison, Monroe, and Adams, also by Clay, Webster, and Everett. He was vestryman of the Episcopal Church, Ballston Spa, and a founder of Saratoga County Bible Society. In 1840 he was elected senator to the legislature of New York. The senate was then the highest court of appeal in that State, and in 1841, while preparing opinions in cases argued in that court, he was stricken with paralysis, permanently disabled, and resigned his senatorial office. He died in 1854 in Cleveland, Ohio, at the home of his eldest daughter and her husband Wil-

liam D. Beattie, where he was tenderly
cared for during the last ten years of his
life. He and his wife are buried in the
cemetery family lot at Ballston Spa. He
was a gentleman of the old school, polite
and courteous, a forcible speaker, and
delivered frequent orations on literary and
national topics. He was a National Repub-
lican and a Whig. In private life he was
retiring, fond of cultivating his garden, and
generous in distributing its fruits and flowers.
He was a Phi Beta Kappa, and delivered
before that society, at Harvard College,
Mass., the commencement oration in 1827.
He accompanied General Lafayette, of
France, through New England, in his last
visit to the United States. He hated cor-
ruption in politics and spurned the use of
money for political personal success, and his
constituency always retained unwavering
confidence in his sterling integrity.

Their children were [6]Sarah Jane, born February, 1808; [6]James Hodge, October, 1809;

[6]Elizabeth Ann, October, 1812; [6]Malvina, March, 1815; [6]John William, February, 1817; [6]Charles Edward, January, 1820; [6]Oscar, February, 1822; [6]Edgar, April, 1824. All born in Saratoga county, N. Y.

[5]ELISHA TAYLOR, youngest son of Judge John Taylor, was born May, 1785, died 1861. From the age of thirteen he supported himself. He was educated in part at Union College. He engaged in mercantile business in Schenectady, about 1807, and married Ann Dunlap in 1810. In 1818 he removed to Cleveland, Ohio, and engaged in mercantile pursuits. His wife died in 1824. He married Elizabeth Ely of Long Meadow, Mass., in 1826, and removed to Cherry Valley, N. Y., where he remained until 1833, when he returned to Schenectady. He became intensely interested in the subject of temperance. Total abstinence from intoxicating liquors was then a new thought. He accepted it and spent ten years of the best of his life in advocating it. Spent his

time. money and vigorous intellect freely
for this object. In 1843 he removed to
Cleveland, Ohio, and engaged in mercantile
pursuits. He made investments in real
estate in and adjoining the cities of Cleveland and Indianapolis, which proved very
advantageous and profitable. He died in
Cleveland, April 23, 1861, leaving a large
estate. He was from early life a consistent
and earnest member of the Presbyterian
Church, and for many years an elder in that
church. He contributed liberally and by
rule (I have been told he gave one-fourth of
his net profits annually for many years) for
benevolence and the spread of the Gospel.
He was an officer in the army in the War of
1812. His children were nine, of whom
three attained lawful age: [6]Alfred, born
April, 1820; [6]Louisa, August, 1822; [6]John
William, June, 1824. All born in Cleveland, Ohio.

[5]ELIZABETH, daughter of Judge John Taylor, was born July 13, 1788 (and is still

living in 1886). She had the best educational advantages the country afforded, and
married Nathan Seeley, a farmer, December
31, 1811. Her husband was drafted as a
soldier in the War of 1812. They resided
in Carlisle, Schoharie county, and Charles-
town, Montgomery county, N. Y. He
became a deacon in the Baptist Church.
Their house was a haven of rest to many a
weary minister of the Gospel, and a very
hospitable home. Her husband died May 5,
1862, at Syracuse, and she has ever since
lived with her eldest son, Rev. John T.
Seeley, D. D., a prominent Baptist clergyman in western New York. Her children
were three sons and two daughters, all of
whom married, to-wit: [6]John T., born January, 1814; [6]Jesse N., May, 1815; [6]Ann
Eliza, June, 1817; [6]David W., January,
1821; [6]Chloe Jane, January, 1825. Mrs.
Seeley—who will be ninety-eight years old
July, 1886, has retained her faculties well
until recently, has good appetite, sleeps well,

but sight and hearing are failing—resides at Pittsford, N. Y., with her son, Rev. Dr. Seeley.

[5]SALLY, daughter of Judge John Taylor, born February 21, 1792 (and still living in 1886), was well educated, energetic and cheerful, though slight and fragile in person. She was married to Daniel Holmes, a farmer, February 12, 1811, and settled in Carlisle, N. Y. In 1813 they united with Presbyterian Church. In February, 1818, they removed to " Holland purchase," Wilson, Niagara county, N. Y., on the shore of Lake Ontario, where she endured the privations, hardships and poverty of frontier life with Christian heroism, equal to every emergency, physical, mental and moral. She was the mother of thirteen children, of whom ten survived and became the heads of families. Her heart and hand were ever open to the sad, sick and needy. She was one of six who, in 1819, organized the First Presbyterian Church of Wilson. To it her

sympathy, prayers and material aid have been constantly and cheerfully given for sixty-seven years. She has given a bountiful thanksgiving dinner to her children and descendants every year for more than fifty years, never neglecting to express her earnest desire for the spiritual welfare of her family to the latest generation. Her brother, Hon. John W. Taylor, in 1845, writes: "She was a favorite sister. To energy and decision she united a mild temper and great industry. She had a place for everything, and everything in its place." Her husband, Daniel Holmes, died May 26, 1858. He was an elder and deacon in the Presbyterian Church at Wilson, and both were greatly beloved by all their acquaintances. When over eighty years old she was relating to a niece many of the incidents of her life and closed thus—"and I think I have enjoyed as much domestic happiness as is often found on earth." Her children who survived were [6]Sarah Ann, born

January, 1812; [6]Richard Cox, December, 1813; [6]John Taylor, December, 1815; [6]Ezra Sprague, July 1819; [6]Elisha Taylor, March, 1824; [6]George Alfred, April, 1826; [6]Mary Elizabeth, September, 1828; [6]James Edward, January, 1831; [6]Daniel, Jr., April, 1833; [6]Lydia Louisa, June, 1837. Mrs. Holmes still occupies the old homestead with her daughter Mary Elizabeth Holmes Brown and family, always ready to welcome the absent members of the family and their friends. She is in good health, writes a beautiful letter, and is an industrious Bible student in 1886.

[5]ANNA, youngest child of Judge John Taylor, was born September, 1794, and died January, 1840. She was a beautiful girl—vivacious, interesting and attractive. She married Ezra Sprague, a merchant, November, 1815. He was unfortunate in business, became discouraged, and had poor health for many years. They had five children: [6]William, born September, 1816, died June,

1842; [6]David, June, 1818, died April, 1836; Mary, September, 1819, married Daniel McDougal, 1845, and died at birth of her daughter, Mary S., in 1846; Anna, April, 1821, married Harvey Smith, September, 1845; and Sarah, March, 1823, died September, 1847, unmarried. Her daughter Anna said of her mother: "She was a dear, noble, loving mother."

### AGED TAYLORS.

JUDGE JOHN TAYLOR was 80 years old. His brother William, 87 years. He had fourteen children by one wife. Eight of these died averaging 85 years. The other six, 90 years. [3]Mercy Cox, nee Taylor, mother of [4]Chloe Cox Taylor, wife of [4]Judge Taylor, died at 99 years. [4]James, cousin of John, died at 90. His son John, at 85. [4]James Cox, brother of [4]Chloe, lived to be 93 years old. [5]Elizabeth, eldest daughter of Judge John Taylor, is yet living,

35

nearly 98 years old. [5]Sally, another daughter, is yet living, 94 years old. Many others have lived beyond threescore and ten years.

GRAND-CHILDREN OF JUDGE JOHN TAYLOR AND GREAT GRAND-CHILDREN.

CHILDREN OF RICHARD TAYLOR, BORN 1777, AND HIS GRAND-CHILDREN.

[6]ANSON HAWLEY TAYLOR, born 1803, married Miss Dennison, had two children, Mary E. and [7]Anson Hawley, Jr.—being deaf he was killed while standing on the railroad track at Joliet, Ill., by a train of cars, about 1864. His business was constructing public works and railroads in New York and in the Western States.

His daughter, [7]Mary E. Taylor, married to Kellogg Sexton of Milwaukee, had four children, of whom two survive, viz., Arthur and Paul. Mr. Sexton is deceased, and his widow is in New England.

[7]ANSON H. TAYLOR, Jr., was in business

with his father. He married Emma Goodwin. They have one child, and their residence is the city of Havana, Cuba, West Indies.

[6]OBADIAH, son of the second wife of Richard Taylor, died nine years old.

[6]JOHN WRIGHT TAYLOR, born 1808, died 1843—three times married. The first two wives died without children. In 1840 he married Mary Bancroft, who had one son, [7]Edward B. Taylor, born August, 1841, and who, in May, 1861, enlisted in the 1st California Regiment at Philadelphia. He lost his left hand in battle of Ball's Bluff, October, 1861; was discharged February, 1862, for disability. In June, 1864, he married Maria S. Newcomb, Philadelphia, removed to Milwaukee, Wisconsin, and in 1869 to Port Huron, Michigan, where he now resides. They have five children: [8]Cornelia, [8]Edith, [8]John Wright, [8]Edward Bancroft, and [8]Paul, born between 1865 and 1875.

[6]CHLOE SOPHIA TAYLOR, only daughter

of [5]Richard Taylor, born May, 1810, married James Callen, November, 1825, purchased the farm and homestead of [4]Judge John Taylor, Charlton, N. Y., where they lived many years. They had thirteen children: [7]Sarah Jane, born September, 1826, lived eight years; [7]John T. Callen, 1828, a teacher in New Jersey; [7]James Edwin Callen, 1830, married Francis Randall—of their three children only one, [8]Anna S. Callen, survives. She is a bright, ambitious girl—a teacher. Her father served three years in the Civil War, and was honorably discharged. [7]Richard Callen, born 1832, married Hattie Parker, who had two children, [8]Aletha and [8]Lizzie. He was a successful teacher for many years, greatly esteemed, and died February, 1865. [7]Sarah Jane Callen, born September, 1834, married to Rev. B. Chadwick of Columbus, Ohio. She is an active Christian in mission work. [7]Elizabeth Ann, born 1838, died 1859; [7]Levi Lorenzo Callen, born February, 1842, married Lottie Beach—had two children, [8]Richard and [8]Lucy. He was a colonel in the Union Army in the Civil War, seriously wounded and honorably discharged. [7]Edward Callen, born 1846, married Caroline Wheeler, had a daughter, [8]Carrie, ~~who died~~. Married second wife, Mrs. White, a widow with one daughter. He is a farmer and justice of the peace. [7]Mary C. Callen, born March, 1848, was married to George H. Barlow, and has three bright boys—[8]Harry, [8]Frank, and [8]James. They reside at Ilion, N. Y. [7]Georgianna Sophia Callen, born June, 1850, married Frank Wheeler. They reside in Schenectady, N. Y.

[6]RICHARD TAYLOR, son of Richard of 1777, and child of his fourth wife, was killed by a falling tree in a whirlwind. [6]Rev. Elisha Ephraim Leech Taylor, D. D., born September 25, 1815, at Pompey, N. Y., graduated from Madison University and Theological Seminary, Hamilton, N. Y., 1840, was called to Brooklyn, N. Y., gathered and

organized the Pierpont Street Baptist Church and was its pastor nine years, resigned, and with some of his congregation formed the Mission, in South Brooklyn, which very soon became "Strong Place Baptist Church," a church of remarkable power and influence. In 1854, their new edifice being completed and Mr. Taylor greatly overworked, his people sent him abroad to Europe for six months. He was pastor of that church until 1864, and, owing to nervous prostration, resigned. His congregation presented him with $20,000 as a slight token of their regard and appreciation, After two years of rest and travel he became Secretary of the "Baptist Church Edifice Fund," and raised for it about $250,000. In 1874 he was made sole secretary of that society, which had for several years required the attention of three officials. He was stricken with typhoid fever in July and died August 18, 1874, at his summer home at Marlboro, on the Hudson, New York.

He married Mary Jane Perkins, daughter
of Aaron Perkins, D. D., in 1840. They
had nine children. In 1873 he married
Mrs. Adra E. Bradbury, who survived him.
He was congenial and forcible, wise and
faithful. As preacher, pastor and secretary
he was successful. His life was richly
blessed. Their children are: [7]Albert Judson, born July 1, 1844; [7]Morgan Smith,
June 11, 1846; [7]James Monroe, August 5,
1848; [7]Charles Herbert, August 9, 1850;
[7]Mary Baxter, May, 1853; [7]Electus Backus
Litchfield, August 22, 1856; [7]Grace, November 5, 1859, died March, 1865; [7]Wm. Elliot,
June 14, 1861, died June 14, 1884; [7]Louise
Kent, November, 1863.

"OF THE CHILDREN OF REV. ELISHA E. L.
TAYLOR, D. D., BORN SEPTEMBER, 1815."

[7]ALBERT JUDSON TAYLOR, born in Brooklyn, N. Y., July 1, 1834, graduated from the
University at Rochester, N. Y., 1864; in

business in New York; married Delia
Stearns, 1868, and died May 5, 1870—one
son, [8]Elisha E. L. Taylor.

[7]MORGAN SMITH TAYLOR, born June 11,
1846; in business in New York since 1865;
married May S. Pike, Calais, Me., 1870.
They have two [8]daughters and one [8]son.
Residence in Plainfield, N. J.

REV. [7]JAMES M. TAYLOR, born August 5,
1848, graduated from University at Rochester, N. Y., 1868, and Theological Seminary, Rochester, 1871. In Europe 1871–2;
pastor at Norwalk, Conn., and Providence,
R, I., from 1873 to 1885. He possesses
great ability and high character. Elected
President of Vassar College, New York, in
1886; married Kate Huntington, Rochester,
1873. Their children are two [8]sons and one
[8]daughter.

[7]CHARLES HERBERT TAYLOR, born August
9, 1850, graduated from University at Rochester, N. Y., 1870; trip to Europe; attorney-
at-law. Entered on business life in New

York. In 1885 was cashier of New York
Custom House. Married Delia S. Taylor,
1883.

7MARY BAXTER TAYLOR, born May 2,
1853, graduated from Vassar College, New
York, 1875; studied medicine in New York;
married Willard T. Bissell, 1876; left a.
widow 1878; renewed study of medicine;
graduated from Medical College, New York,
and is practicing medicine in New York.
President of Vassar College Alumnae,
1884–6. One son, 8Philip Bissell.

7ELECTUS BACKUS LITCHFIELD TAYLOR,
born August 22, 1856; visited Europe 1871;
in college at Rochester, and, by reason of
nervous prostration, did not complete his
course. In business South, and since 1884
member of the Nursery Company, "The
H. E. Hooker Co.," Rochester, N. Y.
Married Caroline Hooker, 1885.

7GRACE TAYLOR, born November 5, 1859,
died 1865.

7WM. ELLIOT TAYLOR, born June 14,

1861; in business in New York; died 1884.
[7]LOUISE HUNT TAYLOR, born November, 1863; teacher. Resides with Morgan S. Taylor, her brother, Plainfield, N. J.

[6]JAMES MONROE TAYLOR, born at Pompey, N. Y., December 13, 1818. Engaged in business for himself while a minor as a dry goods merchant; married Charlotte E. Davis, January 15, 1840. Established the first saleratus factory in the country at Delphi, afterwards at Syracuse, N. Y.; then in Brooklyn, N. Y., and conducts his business in New York city, where he resides, and ranks among the successful business men—characterized by great energy and persistence and boundless hospitality. Of their two children, [7]Laura Maria Taylor graduated at Elmira Female College, New York; married Chas. C. Pope of Syracuse; resides in New York city; have two [8]sons and a [8]daughter, and Mr. Pope is in business with [6]J. Monroe Taylor.

[7]CHARLOTTE TAYLOR, born at Syracuse,

married George Doheny, Esq., of Syracuse, N. Y., and died two years afterwards. No children survive.

### GRAND CHILDREN AND GREAT GRAND-CHILDREN OF JUDGE JOHN TAYLOR.

#### CHILDREN OF [5]WILLIAM TAYLOR, BORN 1779, AND GRAND-CHILDREN.

[6]JAMES EDWIN TAYLOR, born September, 1807,; a bright student and was preparing for college at Cherry Valley Academy, and died there in 1830.

[6]WILLIAM LORENZO TAYLOR, born November, 1808, is a farmer in Charlton; married Lydia Valentine; has one child, [7]William, who married and had a [8]son and [8]daughter. Mr. Taylor visited California, in 1849, but soon returned to his farm and comfortable home. He has been assessor and supervisor of Charlton many years. An energetic man; for a few years had business connections in the city of New York, and now, at the

age of 77, is residing with his wife, his son
and his grand-children on his farm at Little
Troy, Charlton, Saratoga county, N. Y.

⁶EBER LEANDER TAYLOR, born June, 1810,
was a well educated teacher and farmer. In
1833 he married Charlotte Jennings of
Charlton, and removed to Michigan, near
Pontiac, where he cleared up and put under
cultivation two new farms, and resided there
until 1873, when he sold his farms and purchased a farm, grist mill and lumber yard
at Fulton, Bourbon county, Kansas. His
first wife died and was buried at Pontiac.
They had eight children : ⁷William Elliott,
⁷Elisha Otis, ⁷Charles Henry, ⁷James Edwin,
⁷Malvina, ⁷Maria Elizabeth, ⁷Caroline, ⁷Lucy
Jane. He married a second wife after
moving to Kansas. He died and was
buried at Fulton in 1885.

"OF THE CHILDREN OF EBER L. TAYLOR, OF 1810."

⁷WM. ELLIOT TAYLOR married Mary

Hubbell; have one daughter, [8]Carrie; reside in Big Rapids, Mich.; has a farm adjoining the city; loans money, manages estates.

[7]CHARLES H. TAYLOR, attorney-at-law, married and has two [8]children, a [8]son and [8]daughter; reside at South Orange, N. J.; in business in New York. He and J. E. Colby are authors and publishers of new editions of "Adams' Illustrated Chart of History," adding new countries.

[7]JAMER E. TAYLOR, unmarried, in business in Chicago, Ill.

[7]MALVINA TAYLOR, married to John E. Colby, settled in Cleveland, Ohio; had five children. She died in 1875; all of her children have since died.

[7]ELISHA OTIS TAYLOR, born in Pontiac, went to California and Oregon; was engaged several years in managing a mine, and while protecting some of his men from injury was injured himself, and finally died after two years of suffering.

[7]MARIA ELIZABETH TAYLOR, unmarried, a very energetic and efficient teacher in Detroit (travelled four months in Europe in 1878), and now at Cleveland, Ohio.

[7]CAROLINE TAYLOR married Samuel T. Delano, settled at Fulton, Kansas, is in successful and prosperous business. Have [8]three bright, vigorous, intelligent boys.

[7]LUCY JANE TAYLOR married John E. Colby (his second wife); in business in New York city. They are now in Europe for a few months. All the daughters were educated at the female seminaries in Cleveland and Detroit. The boys in Union School, Pontiac, and at the University of Michigan, Ann Arbor.

[6]ANN ELIZA TAYLOR, born February, 1812, died June, 1854. She married Asa Hollister; had no children; resided at Burnt Hills, in Ballston, Saratoga county, N. Y.; had a very pleasant home, and was greatly beloved by all who knew her.

[6]SARAH SOPHIA TAYLOR died an infant.

⁶JOHN TAYLOR, a farmer, born July, 1815, married Susan Wheeler, about 1837, moved to Genesee county, Mich., and resided there until his death, in 1866, at Flint. They had four children : ⁷John Wheeler, ⁷Clarence Linden, ⁷Louisa—all of whom married and had children, ⁸Lewis Edward and ⁸Susan S. and ⁸Eva L. Taylor and ⁸Lulu B. Shelton —and ⁷Sarah, not married. Their mother died about 1867. The two daughters have died since.

⁶ELISHA TAYLOR, born May 17, 1817, graduated from Union College, 1837; Phi Beta Kappa, 1837; teacher at Athens, 1838; attorney-at-law, Detroit, Mich., 1839; city attorney of Detroit, 1843; member of Board of Education, 1843–5; married Aurelia H. Penfield, 1844; master in chancery, 1842–6; register of United States land office, 1843–5; clerk of the supreme court of Michigan, 1848–9; receiver of the United States land office, Detroit, 1853–7; United States agent for paying pensions, 1854–5; judge at cham-

bers, 1846–50; United States depositary of
public monies collected in Michigan, North-
ern Ohio and Indiana, 1853–7; elder in
Jefferson Avenue Presbyterian Church, Detroit, 1856–86; a commissioner to the general assembly of the Presbyterian Church,
1868, at Harrisburg, and in 1884 at Saratoga; compiler of this genealogy. Enough
said.

⁷DE WITT H. TAYLOR, his son, born
August, 1848; educated in the Detroit
Union and High Schools, and at University
of Michigan, 1860–71; and attorney-at-law,
Detroit. In successful mercantile business
three years, and in 1874–5 spent fifteen
months in travels in Europe, Asia, and
Africa. Now in active business in Detroit,
Mich.

⁶SAMUEL TAYLOR, born 1819, was twice
married; died March 4, 1857; left no
children.

⁶DAVID TAYLOR, born 1821, died September, 1833.

[6]RICHARD TAYLOR, born 1823, farmer; elder in the Presbyterian Church, Ballston; married Delia Warren; had five children: [7]Charles, [7]Emma R., [7]Ella, [7]Lucy J. and [7]Asa. [6]He resides at the homestead of his father and mother in Charlton, and cared for his mother in her declining years. She died there at the age of seventy-five years. His wife died in 1880. His daughters are all well educated, successful teachers. His son [7]Charles died at nineteen years of age of malignant scarlet fever. He with his son Asa and one of the daughters keep the hearth fires burning in the homestead of his father, [5]William Taylor of 1779.

[6]JOSIAH TAYLOR, born April, 1825, died April, 1869. He was a farmer in western New York and in Michigan. He was a courageous and efficient soldier in the army of the United States during the War of the Rebellion, and died from the exposure and disease incident to great hardship in the army. He was married and had children

who survive him. [7]Alice, who is married and resides near Poughkeepsie, N. Y., and [7]Helen A., now a student in one of the normal schools in New York.

[6]LUCY JANE TAYLOR, born May, 1827, married Wm. J. Philip, and they removed to Du Page, Wayne county. Ill., on a farm where she died. They had six children: [7]Irving, [7]Edwin, [7]Charles, [7]Herbert, [7]Mary, and [7]Julia. [7]Irving was educated at the college at Wheaton, Ill., and is a Congregational minister. [7]Edwin was educated in part at the University of Michigan, and was admitted to the bar and practices law in the State of Illinois. [7]Charles married and died. [7]Mary married Mr. Sedgwick, and has a large family of [8]children. Her husband was a keeper of one of the United States storehouses at or near Chicago, Ill., for many years, under the internal revenue laws. The family have recently removed to Dakota. Her sister [7]Julia is with her.

[6]JOSEPH ELLIOTT TAYLOR, born 1829,

married Caroline Braut of Ballston, N. Y.,
in 1848, and removed to Michigan and
settled on the bank of one of the beautiful
lakes in Oakland county, where they had a
pleasant farm and home, and were very
hospitable. They had one son, ⁷William,
who married and resides with his mother at
their homestead. ⁶Joseph Elliott died suddenly after six months illness in 1874.

### GRAND-CHILDREN OF JUDGE JOHN TAYLOR AND GREAT GRAND-CHILDREN.

#### CHILDREN OF EDWARD TAYLOR, BORN 1781, DIED 1866, AND GRAND CHILDREN.

⁶John Orville Taylor, born May 14,
1807; graduated at Union College, Schenectady, N. Y., 1830; author of "The
District School; or, Popular Education,"
published by Harper Brothers, New York,
1834—a third edition by Cary & Lee, Philadelphia; married Jane Agnew, November
16, 1835; edited and published "Common

School Assistant," in 1836, having a monthly
circulation of 56,000—after four years it
was adopted and published by the State of
New York; is yet in the editorial chair, in
1886, on a newspaper in New Brunswick,
N. J. Had one son, ⁷Edward, who married,
and died in 1880, leaving a ⁸daughter.

⁶ANN MARIA TAYLOR, born 1810, married
to Solomon Waring. They had seven children: ⁷Richard S., ⁷Orville, ⁷Marietta, ⁷Mel-
vina, ⁷Edward J., and two died young. The
parents have died. The two sons are successful manufacturers of oil, at Pittsburgh,
Pa., and have families. Richard S. invented
"Waring's Underground Cable." Residence, Plainfield, N. J.

⁶LUZERNE CURTIS TAYLOR, born 1812,
farmer, married Hannah Platner. They
had fourteen children—eight boys, six girls:
⁷Eunice, ⁷Edward, ⁷Phineas, ⁷Alfred, ⁷Martha,
⁷Aaron, ⁷John, ⁷Elisha, ⁷Alonzo, ⁷Susan (who
died young), ⁷Phebe, ⁷Walter, ⁷Ida, ⁷Harriet.
Most of them married and have children.

About 1856 they settled near Dunbar, Minn.; mostly farmers. The latest report is thirty-three children of the eighth generation and two grand-children of the ninth generation.

[6]Phebe Eliza Taylor, born 1814, died about 1872, married Rev. Alfred H. Taylor, a Baptist clergyman. He was a chaplain in the Union Army in the Civil War, 1861–5. They had five sons and one daughter. Two survive, [7]Alfred and [7]Edward Judson; both have [8]families. [7]Anna, another child, was married and died, leaving [8]children.

[6]Elisha Cox Taylor, born 1816, married Harriet Hart; had nine children. Three died young. Survivors are [7]Hart, [7]Edward, [7]Orville, [7]Charles, [7]Dennis, and [7]Adrian; mostly married and have children. About 1841 Elisha Cox Taylor settled in or near Annapolis. During the Civil War his property was made the camping ground for both armies at different times, and the products of his large tannery were confis-

cated by both. He has since removed to Baltimore, Md. He has [8]grand-children.

[6]WILLIAM ANDREW TAYLOR, born 1819, married Minerva Jenne, 1842. Had children, some died young. [7]Clarence, who married and has children, resides in Ballston, N. Y., and his [8]children reside in Minnesota.

[6]JANE CAROLINE TAYLOR, born 1821, married to Gilbert Connor, had five children: [7]Mary married to Albert McKnight, and has children; [7]Clara, who died; [7]Edward, [7]William, and [7]Susan.

[6]EMMA CLARA TAYLOR, born 1825, married Alexander Hubbs; died without children.

[6]SARAH ELIZABETH TAYLOR, born 1827, married to Rev. David I. Yerkes, a prominent Baptist clergyman and author, who has been the pastor for more than twenty-three years of the large Baptist Church at Plainfield, N. J. Their children are: [7]Clara, born 1851, married to C. H. Smith; [7]Ida, 1853; [7]Joseph, 1855; [7]Alice, 1861, married

to Walter McGee; [7]Hannah, 1864, married
Wm. Flanders; [7]Grace, 1866. Several other
children died young. She has [8]grand-
children.

[6]SUSAN PATIENCE TAYLOR, born 1830,
married to John R. Wilson, who for twenty-
seven years held an important position in
the Delaware and Hudson River Railroad
Company, at Ballston Spa, N. Y. He died
in 1882. Their son, [7]Edward Taylor, born
January, 1869, is in business in New York.

[6]Phebe, [6]Jane, [6]Eunice, and [6]Sarah, were
married in the same house where their
father and mother were married.

GRAND-CHILDREN OF JUDGE JOHN TAYLOR.

CHILDREN OF JOHN W. TAYLOR, BORN 1784, DIED 1854.

[6]SARAH JANE TAYLOR, born February 27,
1808, and educated at Mrs. Willard's Seminary, Troy, N. Y. In 1825 married William
D. Beattie, born 1802, a graduate of Union

College, Schenectady, N. Y. He was a man of great intelligence and culture, with singular honesty and simplicity of character. In 1838 they removed to Cleveland, Ohio. Ten children were born to them, of whom all but two have died between fifteen and twenty years of age. [7]Mary Jane and [7]Sarah Louise have spent many years in Europe in traveling. They reside in New York or Lakewood, N. J. Their mother died in 1857. Mr. Beattie, in 1861, in New York.

[6]JAMES HODGE TAYLOR, born October 6, 1809, graduated from West Point Military Academy, 1829, and appointed an instructor there; drowned October, 1835 (crossing Cossitot river on horseback), while in the line of his duty in the army, near Fort Towson, Indian Territory. His grave is in the national cemetery at Fort Gibson. He was not married.

[6]ELIZABETH ANN TAYLOR, born October 12, 1812, married May 19, 1843, to Thomas D. Robertson, who became a

prominent banker in Rockford, Ill., and large land holder. Six children; only two survived to mature age. She died May 6, 1878. Her grave is at Rockford, Ill. Surviving children are [7]William Taylor Robertson, banker, Rockford, Ill., who married Edith White, and they have two [8]children; [7]Mary Palmer Robertson, married to David N. Starr, Rockford, traveled four months in Europe in 1878.

[6]MALVINA TAYLOR, born March 9, 1815, graduated at Female Seminary, Ballston Spa; married to Dr. Edward Taylor of Ohio, October 1, 1839. They spent several years in State of Mississippi. They settled in Cleveland, Ohio, where he died in 1868. Her widowhood has been spent with her brothers in the Western States, and recent years in her native Ballston, Saratoga county, N. Y., in usefulness and active Christian work.

[6]JOHN W. TAYLOR, born February 22, 1817, trained for mercantile business in

Albany and New York, removed to Illinois, 1838; married Jane P. Wadleigh, Albany, August 19, 1839; was probate judge of Winnebago county, Ill.; master in chancery and commissioner in bankruptcy in 1856-61, also banker, real estate dealer at Dubuque, Ia., and director and treasurer of school board of that city. In 1861 was appointed captain and served as quartermaster in the Civil War of 1861-5, in Missouri and Mississippi; was promoted to lieutenant-colonel and was chief quartermaster of the Fourteenth Army Corps, and afterwards of the Army of the Cumberland. An honest, faithful and efficient officer. Six children were born, of whom three survive: [7]John Wadleigh, born November, 1840, married Sarah Waxe. They have three [8]children; reside at St. Paul, Minn.; manager of an express company. He was in the Union Army during the War, in Quartermaster's Department. [7]Ella Malvina, born December, 1844, married to William N.

Goddard, who developed remarkable business capacity in New York, but died five years after their marriage, leaving his widow and two [8]children. They reside in Utica, N. Y.

[7]JAMES HODGE TAYLOR, born October 1, 1847, a successful wholesale merchant in New York, married Carrie Beyea; have one [8]child.

[6]CHARLES EDWARD TAYLOR, born January 23, 1820, graduated from Union College, 1839; studied law at Ballston Spa; commenced the practice of his profession in Alabama, and died at Snow Hill, Wilcox county, Ala., September 25, 1847.

[6]OSCAR TAYLOR, born February 16, 1822, at Ballston Spa, N. Y.; went to Rockford in 1839; settled in Freeport, Ill.; was merchant, banker and lawyer; married Martha Malvina Snow, August 2, 1842. She was a graduate of Mrs. Willard's Seminary, Troy, N. Y.; very capable. Six children born to them: [7]Elizabeth Fleming and [7]Mary Mal-

vina (twins), May, 1843—Mary died 1844.
[7]Elizabeth, educated in Philadelphia, married Jerome Maynard, a merchant; had five children — one, [8]Elsie Taylor, survives. Mother died November, 1878. [7]Louise Winnesheck, born February, 1846; well educated; in 1872 founded the Circulating Library of Freeport, and acted as librarian; resides at Freeport with her parents. [7]Oscar Livingston Taylor, born September, 1858, graduated from Cornell University, N. Y., in 1881; married Nora T. West, June, 1885; resides at St. Paul; in real estate business. [7]Clarissa Sarah, born November, 1863, is a pupil of her mother in the art of china painting; residence, Freeport, Ill. [7]Malvina Snow, Jr., died 1862, an infant.

[6]EDGAR TAYLOR, born at Ballston Spa, N. Y., April 11, 1824, graduated in Medical Department of Western Reserve College, Ohio, in 1858, and also from Dental College, Cincinnati, Ohio, 1859. Settled at Palmyra, Mo., where he has since pursued his pro-

fession successfully. Married Mary Tebbs Pepper, October 25, 1860, of Kentucky; educated at Cincinnati Wesleyan College.

GRAND-CHILDREN OF JUDGE JOHN TAYLOR.

CHILDREN OF ELISHA TAYLOR, BORN 1785, DIED 1861, AND HIS GRAND-CHILDREN.

⁶ALFRED TAYLOR, born April, 1820, graduated from Union College, New York, and from Jefferson Medical College, Philadelphia. He practiced medicine and surgery in Ohio. In 1861 he was appointed surgeon (with the rank of major) in the Third Ohio Cavalry, and ordered to Fort Leavenworth, Kansas. In March, 1862, he was transferred to the Army of the Tennessee, and on his way to join his regiment. he was accidentally drowned in the Ohio river, above Louisville. He was drawn overboard from the steamer by the pail and rope when drawing water for his horse. His body was never found.

He married Maria Dewey, May, 1845. She died in 1846. He married Helen A. M. Leonard, November, 1849; had five children, two died young. They resided in Cleveland, in 1860. He stood high in his profession; was a scholarly man, conversant with the best English literature. His surviving children are:

REV. 7FREDERICK WM. TAYLOR, born January, 1853, graduated from Western Reserve University, Ohio, with degrees B. A. and M. A., and from Episcopal Theological Seminary, New York city, degree S. T. B.; a deacon, 1876; a priest, 1877. Spent seven months in Europe, and, since 1878, has been rector of the Episcopal Church at Danville, Illinois. He is an author, a close student, and successful. He married Cora L. Lamb, August 11, 1874. They have four children: 8Philena, 8Bertha, 8Eunice, 8Alfred Kingsley.

7HARRY OR HENRY TAYLOR, born December, 1857, married Millie Smith, in 1878;

have two [8]children. He has been a manufacturer and dealer in furniture and is now
selling iron. Resides in Cleveland, Ohio.
He is a popular man; good salesman.

[7]ELIZABETH OR BESSIE TAYLOR, born
July, 1860; educated in Cleveland, Ohio;
married to W. J. Crawford, January, 1882;
have two [8]children. Reside in Cleveland,
Ohio.

[6]LOUISA TAYLOR, born August 28, 1822,
at Cleveland; well educated, fine mind, a
ready writer. In 1847 she was married to
Horace F. Waite, Esq., then of Maumee,
Ohio, now a prominent lawyer of Chicago,
Ill. She died in 1849.

[6]JOHN WILLIAM TAYLOR, son of Elisha
Taylor of 1785, born June 2, 1824, graduated from Union College, 1843; married
Anna Sexton of Albany, N. Y., 1848, who
died 1849, leaving one child, [7]Anna Louisa,
born October, 1849. He married Clara
Cushing, 1853, of Springfield, Ohio (second
wife), who died 1868. He married Sarah

Belle Cushing of Springfield. in 1871 (third wife). They have one child, [7]Edith; reside in Cleveland, Ohio. [7]Anna Louisa, who graduated at Vassar College, New York, married George W. Lewton, 1873. They have three children : [8]Frederick, [8]Ada, and [8]Jessemine, and reside in Florida. Mr. [6]Taylor was a bank accountant from 1843 to 1868, in Ohio and Missouri, then removed to Cleveland, and ever since has been the active executor and trustee in the management of his father's estate. Intellectual ability with integrity are his characteristics.

## GRAND AND GREAT GRAND-CHILDREN OF JUDGE JOHN TAYLOR.

### CHILDREN AND GRAND CHILDREN OF [5]ELIZABETH SEELEY NEE TAYLOR, BORN 1788, YET LIVING IN 1886.

REV. [6]JOHN TAYLOR SEELEY, D. D., now pastor of Pittsford Baptist Church, New York, born January 5, 1814, graduated from Madison University, New York, 1839, and from Baptist Theological Seminary, Hamilton, N. Y., 1841. Ordained as minister of the Gospel, and married Harriet M. Seeley, September, 1841 ; commenced his pastoral life at Port Richmond, N. Y., and has not been out of the pastorate a single Sabbath since. Has immersed, baptised eleven hundred persons. Married about one thousand persons, and has been an active, sincere and successful Christian.—Minister in Syracuse, Lima, and other important churches in New York. They have two surviving children : 7James Edwin, born June 28, 1843, a physician, educated at the University of Michigan, at Ann Arbor, and New York Homœopathic Medical College, 1866, where he graduated. He was in the United States Navy in 1863, during the Civil War. He married Ida E. Bolles, March 12, 1869. They have one daughter, 8Ida, and reside in Rochester, N. Y.

7HATTIE ADELLA SEELEY, born January 26, 1856, resides with her parents at Pitts-

.ford; is an artist and pursues her profession.

REV. [6]JESSE N. SEELEY, now of Clinton, Iowa, was born May 15, 1815; licensed to preach 1834; next nine years teacher, preacher and student at Granville College, Ohio, and at Baptist University and Theological Seminary, Hamilton, Madison county, N. Y.; home missionary in Iowa, 1843; organized fifteen churches; pastor in eight —losing his voice compelled him to relinquish preaching. Married Sarah H. C. Chesebrook, 1847. She died 1848; afterwards married Agnes J. Scott, went South, had yellow fever, and remained until 1856; then to Illinois, on a farm, where his second wife died May 25, 1857. For third wife married Mrs. Gulaelma W. Pier, April 3,. 1860. Only five children survive; [7]Adelaide, born December, 1860, now a teacher at Clinton, Iowa; [7]Oscar Judson, born September, 1854, a teacher at Cordova, Ill.; [7]John Wm., born February 7, 1850, in sewing machine business at Burlington, Iowa—married Phebe A. McWhirt, June, 1874. They have four daughters: [8]Ethel, [8]Elma, [8]Nora, [8]Flora.

[7]EMMA ELIZABETH SEELEY, born January, 1853, married to Samuel Marshall, November, 1876. They are farmers, reside near Sauk Rapids, Minn., and have two children: [8]Hattie Elizabeth, born July, 1878; [8]Jessie Adelaide, September 23, 1882.

[7]JESSIE ELMA, born October 10, 1871, with parents; attending school at Clinton, Iowa.

[6]ANN ELIZA SEELEY, born June, 1817, married Rev. T. G. Lamb; died three years thereafter.

[6]DAVID W. SEELEY, born January, 1821, married Maria Loucks; in business in Albany, N. Y. They have three sons: [7]John N., [7]William, a physician, educated in part in the Medical Department of the University of Michigan, Ann Arbor; and [7]Harvey, an engineer.

[6]CHLOE JANE SEELEY, born January, 1825, married Matthew Freeman, an editor. They had five children, to-wit: [7]Elizabeth Freeman, who married Alfred Widener, a farmer; [7]John W. Freeman, who married and is an editorial reporter; [7]Charles Freeman, who married and lives in Ohio; [7]Anna Bell Freeman, who married George Morris. They had three [8]children when Mr. Morris died, and his widow is a teacher; [7]Hattie Freeman, who married Joseph Kelly. They have three [8]children.

GRAND-CHILDREN OF JUDGE JOHN TAYLOR.

CHILDREN OF MRS. SALLY HOLMES NEE TAYLOR, BORN 1792, YET LIVING.

[6]SARAH ANN HOLMES, born January 19, 1812, finished her education at Cazenovia, N. Y., in April, 1829; married Nathaniel Davis of Wilson, Niagara county, N. Y., a farmer. Children were three daughters, six

sons. Two of the sons died from disease in Union Army the first year of the Civil War. Mrs. Davis died October, 1864, and her husband in 1883.

[6]RICHARD COX HOLMES, born December 21, 1813; a successful farmer; supervisor of his town; an elder for forty years in the Presbyterian Church of Wilson. On October 30, 1839, he married Betsey C. Frost, who died March, 1870. They have two [7]sons married and settled in business. In December, 1871, Mr. Holmes married Annista M. Loomis (second wife). They now reside in Lockport, N. Y.

[6]JOHN TAYLOR HOLMES, now Judge of the Police Court of Grand Rapids, Mich., was born December 11, 1815. He was educated in part at Cherry Valley Academy, New York. On March 31, 1836, he married Mary A. Pratt, at Wilson. In 1837 they removed to Grand Rapids, Mich.; engaged in mercantile pursuits, then studied law, was admitted to practice as attorney

and counsellor about 1843; was successful, always sustaining his character and reputation for integrity. He was considerate, kind and genial, with many warm personal friends. In 1875 he was elected Judge of the Superior Court of the city of Grand Rapids, for six years, and twice elected Judge of the Police Court of that city—once, in 1886, as an independent candidate, nominated by the substantial and worthy citizens only two days before the election, and triumphantly elected. Mr. and Mrs. Holmes, on March 31, 1886, celebrated the fiftieth anniversary of their marriage, received a large number of their friends, and were remembered with many tokens of regard, friendship and love. Two daughters and one son are living. Four children have died.

⁶Wm. Edward Holmes, born 1817, died 1824.

⁶Ezra Sprague Holmes, born July 15, 1819, a genius; educated at Oberlin, Ohio, for two years; a musician, a photographer,

a practical skillful dentist, constructing many of the instruments he uses. President for many years of the "Michigan State Sportsmens' Association." October 16, 1852, he married Orianna E. Robbins. One son died; one daughter now living.

[6]JAMES LEANDER HOLMES, born 1822, died 1824.

[6]ELISHA T. HOLMES, born March 21, 1824; educated at Wilson Collegiate Institute; a musician; married Ada Davenport, January 2, 1849; married Caroline E. Barnard, January 1, 1874 (second wife). Three daughters and one son survive: [7]Chloe A., [7]Rose M., [7]Sallie, and [7]David. Two others have died.

[6]GEORGE ALFRED HOLMES, born April 7, 1826. He was in First New York Artillery during the Civil War; was very ill at Fairfax Seminary Hospital, honorably discharged, and receives a pension. He married Elizabeth Remele, January 17, 1850, Their children died young. He was a very skillful horseman.

[6]MARY ELIZABETH HOLMES, born September 25, 1828; educated in Wilson, was married to James G. O. Brown, May 30, 1849; a farmer. They moved into the homestead and took charge of her father's farm in 1854, where they have remained for more than thirty years. Her aged mother has been in the same house with her and has received from Mr. and Mrs. Brown and their family the kindest and most thoughtful consideration and care all these years. They have a family of eight children, two daughters and six sons, two of whom are twins: [7]Mary Elizabeth, [7]Joseph Elmer and [7]David Elsworth, [7]Lewellyn Holmes, [7]Edward Delavan, [7]Sarah Lillian, [7]James Glen, and [7]Samuel Dix.

[6]JAMES EDWARD HOLMES, born January 27, 1831, was educated for a druggist and engaged in that business in Lockport, N. Y., but in 1857 he removed to Iowa. He was a worthy and popular young man and was elected and re-elected for ten years clerk of

the county of Jackson, Iowa, and clerk of the courts, which office he administered to the satisfaction of the public. He was then elected clerk of the Supreme Court of Iowa for two terms. His health failing, he refused another re-election. He married Sarah C. Hyde, October 18, 1853. They have one son and one daughter: [7]Harry, born January, 1861; [7]Hattie E., August, 1867.

[6]DANIEL HOLMES, JR., born April 13, 1833. He engaged in mercantile business in 1854 at Youngstown, N. Y. In 1855 he married Laura R. Spencer. In 1864 he and his family removed to Cleveland, Ohio, where he has been engaged in several kinds of business. They have eight children living: [7]Josephine, [7]Luthella, [7]Lincoln, [7]Tallcot, [7]Edward, [7]Beattie, [7]Florence, [7]Arthur. Two others died.

[6]LUCY JANE HOLMES, born February 11, 1835, died November, 1849. Her sudden decease was a very great affliction to the

family and friends. She was a bright, beautiful and attractive girl.

[6]LYDIA LOUISA HOLMES, born June 6, 1837, enjoyed and improved her educational opportunities, and was a good scholar. After the death of her father, May 26, 1858, she and her mother continued to keep house in the homestead at Wilson, until April 2, 1861, when she was married to Martin C. Brazee, Esq., an ambitious young lawyer of Rockford, Ill., who was also a colonel in the Union Army in the Civil War, 1861–5. Her home was in Rockford from 1861 to 1883, where she died—grievously lamented by a very large circle of dear friends. She was efficient, intelligent, active in every good work, and loved and esteemed by all who knew her. She left surviving three daughters and one son. Her husband ranks high in his profession in Illinois. Her children are: [7]Mary Elizabeth, born April 21, 1870; [7]Kate Lillian, July 22, 1872; [7]Caroline Louisa, November

15, 1874; [7]Martin Holmes, September 24, 1877.

## THE GRAND-CHILDREN OF MRS. [5]SALLY HOLMES NEE TAYLOR. OF 1792.

### CHILDREN OF MRS. [6]SARAH ANN HOLMES DAVIS, BORN 1812.

[7]SARAH MARIA DAVIS, born May 31, 1830, married Jabez S. Woodward, June 1, 1854, a farmer, hardware merchant, editor and proprietor of the *Rural New Yorker*; residence, Lockport. They have two daughters and one son. The eldest of these, [8]Sarah, born 1857, married Thomas McCombe, 1880, and has two [9]sons, being the ninth generation.

[7]SAMUEL DAVIS, born December 14, 1831, married Proxey Barnes, November, 1856. He entered the Union Army, December 16, 1862, and died at Lagrange, Tenn. One [8]daughter survives.

[7]NATHANIEL EMMONS DAVIS, born January 21, 1834. He was well educated as a

civil engineer. He was in the Union Army,
was taken prisoner and suffered untold hor-
rors in Libby and Andersonville prisons.
He secreted some money on his person,
with this he saved his life, but it was long
before he recovered from the effects of the
cruel and barbarous treatment he there
endured. He is a farmer at Fairburg,
Nebraska. He married Harriet Elizabeth
Holden, December 1, 1869. They have
four ⁹children—three sons, one daughter.

⁷HENRY M. DAVIS, born December 13,
1835; teacher, professor, farmer, justice and
lawyer, in Wilson, N. Y.; married Christine
Turner, 1875. ⁸Fred and ⁸Jessie are the
living children.

⁷ELIZA DAVIS, born January 15, 1838,
died May 15, 1859, of fever, in full vigor
of young and accomplished womanhood.

⁷DANIEL. H. DAVIS, born April 14, 1839.
The first in his town to volunteer when
President Lincoln called for 75,000 men to
quell the rebellion in 1861. He was in the

28th New York Infantry. He died May 14, 1862, of fever, in a field hospital, and his body was taken home to Wilson by a comrade, and amid sadness and gloom he was the first soldier buried in his native town.

[7]Mary Elizabeth Davis, born January 26, 1842; married April 26, 1864, to George W. Perrigo. They have three daughters and two sons. They are educated in ways of righteousness. [8]Sarah A., [8]Elizabeth A., [8]Wm. George, [8]Henry L., and [8]Mabel, all born between 1865 and 1880.

[7]Luther Crocker Davis, born October 3, 1846; educated at Wilson Collegiate Institute, married Amanda E. Foot, January 1, 1871, who died May 18, 1874, at Fairburg, Nebraska, leaving [8]Cora, born February, 1872. He married his second wife, Marietta Babcock, February 7, 1877. They have two daughters and one son: [8]Marietta, [8]Bertha, and —.

[7]Wm. Edward Davis, born August 2, 1850; educated at Wilson and at Commer-

cial College, Poughkeepsie, N. Y., was railroad ticket agent at Hannibal, Mo., several years, and is now assistant-general ticket agent of Chicago and Grand Trunk Railroad Company. Married Mary Long, March 17, 1870. They have one son, [8]Wm. E., born 1871.

CHILDREN OF [6]RICHARD COX HOLMES, OF 1813.

• [7]Wm. Howard Holmes, born October 22, 1840; educated at Wilson Collegiate Institute. He entered the Union Army, 1861, in a cavalry company. In 1862 he joined Battery M of First New York Artillery. He served through the War, was in the battles of Winchester, Cedar Mountain, second Bull Run, Antietam, Chancellorville, Gettysburg, and others. In 1863 his division was ordered to Chattanooga, and his battery had their full share of fighting. They were part of Sherman's army through

Georgia to the sea. He returned home at the close of the War unharmed in person and unsullied in character. He has been a teacher; organizer of the Grand Army of the Republic; commander of a Post; deacon in the Presbyterian Church of Wilson, and farmer. He married Jennie Pettit, November 7, 1867, who died August 5, 1877. On March 24, 1881, he married his second wife—Mary E. Tenbrook. They have two [8]sons.

[7]RICHARD PAYSON HOLMES, born October 10, 1849; educated at Wilson. Settled at DeValls Bluff, Arkansas; married Mary E. Seeley, October 25, 1872. They have one son, [8]Richard V., born 1873. Business, raising cattle and other stock. Is social, jovial, shrewd and judicious.

CHILDREN OF JUDGE [6]JOHN T. HOLMES, OF 1815.

[7]MARIETTA HOLMES, born May 22, 1843; married December 4, 1867, to Leonard C.

Remington. Their children are: [8]Mary E., born October, 1869; [8]Lewellyn, March, 1872; [8]Hellen L., January, 1874; [8]Arthur, December, 1879. Two others have died. Mr. Remington entered the Union Army 1862, was in many battles. Had six horses shot under him and his clothing shot; several times ordered to surrender; was never wounded; never a prisoner. He was one of the Company which captured Jeff. Davis, on May 10, 1865. He rode Davis' horse to Macon, Ga., and kept guard over Davis the first night. Mr. Remington is a merchant at Grand Rapids, Mich.

[7]ELIZABETH A. HOLMES, born July 27, 1848; educated at Grand Rapids; residing at home with her parents and brother.

[7]JOHN TAYLOR HOLMES, Jr., born November 22, 1853; is in business in Grand Rapids, in tobacco in its various forms, and resides with his parents.

Four children have died: [7]Daniel E., [7]Augustus, [7]Edwin, and [7]Lewellyn.

CHILD OF ⁶EZRA SPRAGUE HOLMES, OF 1819.

⁷JENNIE WRIGHT HOLMES, born December 27, 1867. Studious and enjoying her opportunities to acquire an education in Grand Rapids, Mich. One son died in 1863—⁷Frederick R.

CHILDREN OF ⁶ELISHA T. HOLMES, OF 1824.

⁷CHLOE AURELIA HOLMES, born December, 1851, was married to John Strong.
⁷ROSE M. HOLMES, born July, 1854, was an excellent teacher, and on November 24, 1881, was married to Lucius Lombard, a merchant in Olcott, N. Y.
⁷SALLIE L. HOLMES, born October, 1874; ⁷Daniel Holmes, October 1876; children of second wife. Two children died.

CHILDREN OF ⁶MARY ELIZABETH HOLMES BROWN, OF 1828.

⁷EDWARD DELEVAN BROWN, born Decem-

ber 23, 1850, married Cordelia Mahoney, March 2. 1884; reside at Fairburg, Nebraska; a farmer.

[7]SARAH LILLIAN BROWN, born November 2, 1854; married, November 16, 1880, R. Stanley Wilson, and moved to Wilks, Montana; one [8]daughter.

[7]JAMES GLEN BROWN, born December 22, 1857. Now in Dubuque, Iowa. Attorney-at-law; a member of the law firm with whom he studied; good abilities, bright prospects.

[7]MARY ELIZABETH BROWN, born March 1, 1860; a teacher at Wilson, N. Y.

[7]JOSEPH ELMER BROWN and [7]DAVID ELSWORTH BROWN (twins), born June 2, 1862. School teachers in Nebraska. Own homestead farms; good habits, good prospects.

[7]LEWELLYN HOLMES BROWN, born October 3, 1868; cultivates bees for honey.

[7]SAMUEL DIX BROWN, born September 29, 1870; at school and assists on the farm at Wilson, N. Y.

CHILDREN OF [6]JAMES E. HOLMES, BORN 1831.

[7]HARRY PORTER HOLMES, born January 21, 1861; educated at Des Moines, Iowa; is a practical silversmith and jeweler. Married Ada Overmore, April 22, 1884.
[7]HATTIE ELIZABETH HOLMES, born August 13, 1867; at school.

CHILDREN OF [6]DANIEL HOLMES, JR., BORN 1833.

[7]LAURA JOSEPHINE HOLMES, born September 19, 1856—a teacher at Cleveland, Ohio; [7]Elizabeth Luthella Holmes, born December 21, 1857—a teacher at Cleveland, Ohio; [7]Rufus Lincoln Holmes, born April 22, 1860—a book-keeper, at Cleveland, Ohio; [7]Albert Talcott Holmes, born July 5, 1862—attorney-at-law, Cleveland; [7]Edward Elisha Taylor Holmes, born October, 1866—a student in school; [7]Beattie Jane Holmes, born April 16, 1869—at School in Cleveland; [7]Florence Lucy Spencer Holmes, born Jan-

uary 1, 1872—at school; [7]Arthur Dearborn
Lord, born June 6, 1876—at school.

---

At their decease, the bodies of Judge
[4]John Taylor, his wife, [4]Chloe Cox Taylor,
her mother, [3]Mercy Cox, and his sister,
[4]Lydia Porter, were buried in the Presbyterian churchyard and burying ground in
Charlton village, Saratoga county, N. Y.,
where the remains are.

## ESCUTCHEON.

THE CREST: A dexter arm, embowed, in armor—the hand in a gauntlet, grasping a javelin. The first and fourth quarters are the Taylor part—white ground, the upper part dark, on which are two wild boars heads. Second quarter, a chevron of ermine between three greyhounds running: for De Fairsted. Third quarter, a chevron of ermine between three rowels of a spur: for Freeland.

MOTTO: *Consequitor quodcunque petit*—
"He accomplishes what he undertakes."

NOTE.—Fifty years ago, Hon. [5]John W. Taylor, of 1784, began collecting facts for a Genealogy. His daughter, Mrs. M. T., has procured the history of the later generations, and is indebted to members of the Taylor, Seeley, and Holmes families for valuable information. [5]Asher Taylor, deceased, of Jersey City, N. J., a descendant of George, the second son of the Emigrant, for more than forty years made a record of all he could learn about the Taylor families, and had a manuscript volume of the size of Webster's Unabridged Dictionary. The compiler has condensed the history gathered from these and other sources.                                              E. T.

DETROIT, May, 1886.

## ADDENDA.

Page 34.

[5]ANNA AND EZRA SPRAGUE family: [7]Mary
S., born 1846, daughter of McDougal, married Spencer A. Brown, Chicago, Ill., lumber
dealer; had two children—[8]Spencer, in 1877,
and [8]Gladye, in 1884.

[6]ANNA, wife of Harvey Smith, had a child,
[7]Sarah, born 1849, who married Thomas H.
Spann, 1872. They had two children, [8]Anna
and [8]Louisa.

---

## ERRATA.

Page 9.—Mathew is spelled with one "t" in all records relative to him.

Page 25.—Gloverville should read Gloversville.

Page 40.—Louise *Kent* should read Louise Hunt.

Page 46.—James should read James.

Page 51.—Wm. J. Philip should read Wm. J. Philips.

Page 65.—Missouri should read Wisconsin.

9 7 8 3 3 3 7 7 3 5 6 9 2